THE MOSCOW
SUBWAY BY Y. ABAKUMOV

THE MOSCOW SUBWAY

By E. ABAKUMOV

DEPUTY TO THE SUPREME SOVIET OF THE U.S.S.R.
CHIEF ON THE MAIN MINE CONSTRUCTION DEPARTMENT
AND MEMBER OF THE COLLEGIUM OF THE PEOPLE'S
COMMISSARIAT OF THE FUEL INDUSTRY ORDER OF LENIN

FOREIGN LANGUAGES PUBLISHING HOUSE
MOSCOW 1939

Artist: B. Schwartz

Printed in the Union of Soviet Socialist Republics

ORTY years ago, in 1899, thirty-nine years after the first municipal underground railway had been built in London, Moscow received its first electric street cars. Up to that time the horse car and the slow droshki had been the city's principal means of public transport.

The question of building a subway in Moscow was first broached at the end of the 19th century. A Russian engineer in the employ of an American firm approached the Moscow City Duma (municipal council) with the proposition of building an underground railway. At that time, however, the city had neither the forces nor the means to carry into effect such a big project, and the Duma was unwilling to hand over so profitable an enterprise to foreign concessionaries. Another reason was that the city fathers of that time owned large plots of real estate in the center of the city and they were afraid that the building of a subway, which would bring the outskirts of the city closer to the center, would cause the value of their property to drop. The result was that the City Duma rejected the proposition.

Up to the Great October Socialist Revolution of 1917 the street cars and droshkis remained the principal means of transportation in Moscow.

After 1917 new industrial establishments employing hundreds of thousands of workers, technicians and engineers sprung up in the former outskirts and suburbs of Moscow. The population of Moscow has more than doubled since 1917. Blocks of new houses and parks have replaced the empty lots and garbage dumps of what recently were the outskirts of the city. The territory of the

6

The Moscow Subway, "Sokel" Station

Soviet capital has spread beyond the former city limits.

At the same time there has been a sharp rise in the "mobility" of the Moscow population. The Moscovite has begun to attend moving picture and theater shows more regularly and has become a frequent visitor to the museums and libraries. The average number of trips per inhabitant increased from 145 in 1913 to 328 in 1929.

Naturally, the street car system—even though it has been reconstructed and considerably enlarged since the revolution—has been unable to cope with the steadily increasing demand for transportation facilities. Neither could this problem be solved by the rapidly growing automobile traffic. With the narrow Moscow streets converging like radii toward the center, the increased automobile traffic has brought about traffic jams on the central thoroughfares.

Thus the problem of urban transportation in Moscow could be solved only by the introduction of a new type of transportation—the underground railway. And in the summer of 1931 the Soviet Government

9

passed a decision to build a network of subway lines in Moscow of a total length of 155 miles.

The decision provided for the building of 46.5 miles of subway lines in fifteen years. A term of three years was fixed for the building of the 7.15 miles of the first section, the construction of which was to start in 1932.

The prospects presaged by the geological investigations made along the route of the first section of the subway were far from cheering. The investigations revealed that in no other city in the world had the subway builders been confronted with such a variety of difficulties as those that faced the future builders of the Moscow subway.

The engineers who built the subway in Berlin had to contend with water-bearing soil. In Paris the uneven surface presented a serious difficulty. In London it was the chaotic arrangement of the underground installations, and in Madrid the medieval lay-out and the crookedness of the streets. In Moscow the subway builders have been confronted with all these difficulties: crooked streets, a dense network of underground installations, remnants of the ancient town, a surface intersected with hills and valleys, and treacherous water-bearing strata.

The volume of work that awaited the subway builders was enormous. The building of the first section alone involved the excavation of about 90,000,000 cu. ft. of earth, the pouring of 30,000,000 cu. ft. of concrete and ferro-concrete, the construction of thirteen underground stations and seventeen vestibules.

A hard and strenuous struggle with nature awaited the builders.

The Central Committee of the Bolshevik Party called upon the entire country to take part in building the subway of the capital.

The country eagerly responded to the call. Scores of thousands of people flocked to Moscow from all ends of the vast Soviet Union.

The Moscow factories delegated their best workers to help in the building of the subway. The Young Communist League and Communist Party organizations at the Moscow mills and factories carried out a voluntary recruiting campaign among their membership. As a result 12,000 young workers went to work on the construction.

Moscow workers, miners from the Donbas, men and women who had worked on the construction of Magnitogorsk, of the Dnieper Dam, of the new railroads, former textile workers, milkmaids, office workers, fitters, seamstresses, candy makers—all met in the excavations of the Moscow subway.

When the work was at its height, there were 65,000 workers on the job. They were men and women of a hundred different trades and professions. But none of the 65,000 had ever worked on the building of an underground railway; the Moscow subway was the first ever to be built in the country.

While not for a moment slowing down the work, it was necessary to fathom the secrets and grasp the fine points of the job in the course of the work itself. It was in the tunnels of the Moscow subway that the scores of thousands of workers were mastering the technique of a job that was entirely new and unknown to them.

Today we can boldly say that the build-

"Dynamo" Station Entrance Pavilion

ers of the Moscow subway have mastered the best of what the world practice of subway building can offer.

They have learned to freeze the soil—to transform an underground quagmire into a solid frozen mass. They have treated the soil with chemical compositions turning wet sand into solid rock. They have mastered the most perfect method of tunneling—by shields.

Forty tunneling shields—all built in one year in Soviet factories—were used simultaneously during the construction of the second section of the subway. Nowhere else in the world have shields been used on such a scale in tunneling work. In England, where the shield was invented, only 22 shields were employed in the building of the last line of the London underground railway.

The entire Soviet Union has taken part in the building of the Moscow subway. The Kuznetsk Stalin Works in Siberia has supplied the subway with rails. Karelia, the Caucasus, the Crimea and the Urals have sent their marble. Chuvashia and the Northern Region have supplied timber. The

Volga districts and the North Caucasus have consigned cement. Moscow, Kharkov, Leningrad have provided the subway with electric motors, complex instruments and equipment. They have also built its escalators—the first in the Soviet Union. Three of these escalators are the longest in the world.

At the time the construction of the Moscow subway was started the Moscow organization of the Bolshevik Party was headed by L. M. Kaganovich—a man of extraordinary energy and great organizational talent, one of J. V. Stalin's closest associates.

L. M. Kaganovich kept in constant touch with the work. He was frequently seen in the subterranean excavations where he spoke to the workers and engineers, gave them advice and inspired the whole body of workers in their struggle against the difficulties that had to be overcome. In view of his great part in this work, the entire body of the subway builders and numerous other organizations requested of the Soviet Government that the Moscow

16

subway be named after L. M. Kaganovich. This request was granted.

Three years after the work had begun the trains of the first section of the Moscow subway were speeding under the streets and squares of the capital. It took another three years to build the second section of the subway, which was completed in the middle of 1938.

The building of the second section of the subway involved the excavation of more than 70,000,000 cu. ft. of earth, and the laying of 215,000 tons of iron tubings and 22,600,000 cu. ft. of concrete; 323,000 sq. ft. of polished marble and granite were used for the facings of the nine stations of the second section of the subway.

Thus, in the course of six years 16.45 miles of subway line have been built in Moscow. This represents an unusually rapid rate of construction. Thus, the building of 34 miles of subway lines in Rome is planned to take 25 years, and that of 15.5 miles of subway lines in Prague is scheduled to take 20 years.

At present work is in full swing on the

construction of the third section of the Moscow subway. Its length will be 8.7 miles, and it is scheduled to be completed by the end of 1940.

Every evening the letter *M* flashes brightly in red neon lights over the street entrances to the Moscow subway (*Metro*).

Stairs of grey and pink granite lead down to the halls. The walls of the short corridor are covered with white polished glass. The many-colored flagstones on the floor are laid out in a mosaic of various designs.

The ceiling in the hall is supported by marble columns. The walls are faced with marble slabs. Three escalators lead down to the platform. They are separated by polished walnut banisters. When the passenger comes down, his eye meets the grand vista of the subterranean station.

The width of the platforms in the underground stations ranges from 32.8 to 69 ft. Thanks to the great width there is no overcrowding on the platforms even in rush hours.

18

"Mayakovsky Square" Station

The underground stations are air-conditioned. Powerful ventilators change the air in the stations from eight to nine times an hour. The air of the Moscow subway is maintained at an even temperature and is always pleasant and pure.

The train, made up of long streamlined cars with plate glass windows, glides into the station. Each train carries about 1,500 passengers. But there is no crowding or crushing during stops. Each car is provided with three automatic double doors.

The train starts. From the windows of the cars one can see the gray walls of the tunnel. The ceiling cannot be seen, because the tunnel lamps are darkened at the top, lighting only the roadbed and the rails. Experience has shown that this lighting arrangement is the most convenient for the motorman.

The diameter of the tunnel is 18.04 ft. This makes the Moscow subway tunnel wider than any other subway tunnel in the world. The building of such tunnels necessarily involved a larger amount of work and greater cost. But it made it possible to use larger and more comfortable cars, and the main concern of the builders of the Moscow subway was to provide the maximum comfort for the passengers.

The rails are welded at their joints, which lessens the noise. The absence of sharp turns (the minimum radius of curvature is 1,970 ft.) ensures the smooth and easy movement of the cars, adding to the comfort of the passengers.

The subway trains run underground the entire length of their way. On the existing lines there is only one place where the subway trains come out on the surface—in crossing the Moscow river over a specially built bridge. But they never run like an elevated railway over the streets of the city.

The stations of the subway have each their individual appearance. No two stations are alike either in architectural design, or in the character of their facings, or in the color effects of the marble, or even in the design of the lighting fixtures. Thirteen different kinds of marble were used on the six stations of the Gorky Street

22

line alone—a distance of six miles. These marbles come from the Urals and Armenia, the Far East and Georgia, Uzbekistan and Siberia.

Foreign visitors are unanimous in their opinion that the Moscow subway is the best in the world.

This is natural and as it should be. For the Soviet people are building the subway system of their capital not as a commercial proposition designed to yield profit to its owners. The people are building the subway for themselves and future generations. The subway is designed to be an integral part of the new Moscow which is being reconstructed with a view to providing the most complete satisfaction of the material and cultural requirements of the population.

Millions of people will use the Moscow subway daily. The subway is so designed and constructed as not to constitute an indispensable daily burden for the passengers, but to combine the maximum comfort with the greatest speed. That is why the tunnels of the Moscow subway are so

23

wide, its cars so comfortable, its "climate" so even and pure, and its stations so beautiful and magnificent.

The Moscow subway is widely used and its popularity is steadily growing. In 1937 the subway carried 155,000,000 passengers. In February 1939 the average number of passengers carried daily exceeded 800,000. It is expected that by the end of 1939 the subway will carry daily 1,500,000 passengers.

These 1,500,000 passengers will be saving daily at least 750,000 hours which they would have had to spend additionally on the slower means of transportation offered by the street cars and autobuses.

The building of the Moscow subway represents another manifestation of the great concern and solicitude for the individual which permeates every phase of construction in the Soviet Union.

Made in the USA
Lexington, KY
12 August 2012